100% ME

DK PUBLISHING

LONDON, NEW YORK,
MELBOURNE, MUNICH, and DELHI

Written and edited by Elinor Greenwood and Alexander Cox
Design Claire Patané, Rachael Smith, Clémence de Molliens, Hedi Gutt, Gemma Fletcher,
Sadie Thomas, Emma Forge, Tom Forge, and Clare Harris

Production editor Sean Daly
Jacket designer Jess Bentall
Jacket editor Mariza O'Keeffe
Design manager Rachael Foster
Publishing manager Bridget Giles
US editor Margaret Parrish
UK consultant Mary-Jo Hill
US consultant Michelle Hainer

First published in the United States in 2009 by DK Publishing
375 Hudson Street, New York, New York 10014

Copyright © 2008 Dorling Kindersley Limited

09 10 11 12 13 10 9 8 7 6 5 4 3 2 1
AD352—10/08

ISBN: 978-0-7566-3470-4 (Hardcover)
978-0-7566-3469-8 (Paperback)

Color reproduction by MDP, United Kingdom. Printed and bound by
Leo Paper Products Ltd., China

Discover more at
www.dk.com

The publisher would like to thank the following for their kind permission to reproduce their photographs:
(Key: a–above; b–below/bottom; c–center; f–far; l–left; r–right; t–top)

Alamy Images: Elmtree Images 57cra; Foodfolio 42cr, 94br; D. Hurst 42bl; Mode Images Limited / Richard Gleed 28–
29 (background). **Corbis:** Darama 74cl; Peter M. Fisher 51bl; Lawrence Manning 26 (background), 27 (background), 76
(background), 77 (background); Mika / Zefa 88–89; Redlink 49clb; Emma Rian / Zefa 34r; Gregor Schuster / Zefa 30–31
(background). **DK Images:** Simon Brown 41fbl. **Getty Images:** Photographer's Choice / Jacobs Stock Photography
17crb; Photonica / Gregor Schuster 8–9b, 62–63b; Riser / Tom Fowlks 82–83; Science Faction / William Radcliffe 58c,
59c; Stone / Francesco Reginato 74t (background); Stone / Tim Flach 9tr, 63tr; Stone+ / Matthias Clamer 72–73; Taxi /
Andy Reynolds 84–85; Taxi / Walter Wick 66c. **Carrie Love:** 44l, 45r. **PunchStock:** Corbis 32–33, 52–53; Digital Vision
/ B2M Productions 51br; Digital Vision / Jessica Wedvick 61cb, 94fbl; Pixland 21tc, 36bl; Stockbyte 6–7 (background),
38–39 (background), 60–61 (background). **Science Photo Library:** John Bavosi 55c, 95bl. **Shutterstock:** 3d_kot 86
(buttons); 78br; Aliciahh 86bl, 86br, 86cla, 86clb, 86cra, 86crb; Michael D. Brown 87br, 87tl; Drawperfect 58bl, 58cl, 59cl;
Fee Graphic 96; Christos Georghiou 59br; Viktor Gmyria 87clb; Sabri Deniz Kizil 12cra; Georgijevic Miroslav 48clb;
Monkey Business Images 4bl; NatUlrich 18tr, 19tr; Pepita 57fcla.
All other images © Dorling Kindersley. For further information see: www.dkimages.com

100% girl 6–37

100% me 38–59

100% boy 60–91

3

Foreword

I can still remember the first time I learned how babies are really made. I was nine years old and a bunch of my girlfriends were over for a pool party. One of them had just gotten a book on the subject and proceeded to describe the whole process, in great detail, to the rest of us. The sun had begun to go down, and our fingers and toes had started to shrivel in the way they often did after spending hours in the pool, but not one of us dared get out of the water. We were riveted by our first "sex" talk. And boy was it informative! Not only did I learn how babies are created, but I also found out that in a few years I'd start getting something called a period, which would cause me to bleed for a week every month. Eww! I was totally grossed out and so embarrassed that it took me weeks to ask my mom if all of this were true. I could barely listen to her answer, even though she assured me that one day menstruation, and even sex, would be a normal part of life.

Well, as was most often the case, my mother was right. I did get used to all of the changes my body was about to go through, and you will too. It didn't happen over night, and I sure didn't love all of it (especially the zits and the body hair that sprouted in weird places) but growing up is a natural stage of life that we all go through. So if you feel awkward or moody or like you'll never fit in, chances are your classmates and friends feel exactly the same way (even the ones who never seem to have a bad hair day). And when all that growing up is done, you might even start to like whatever it was that made you feel awkward in the first place. Hopefully this book will make things easier, whether you read it yourself, or get the details from a friend the way I did—hanging out by the pool on a sunny, summer afternoon.

Michelle Hainer
U.S. Consultant

How to use this book

Girls and boys are different, and they go through puberty in different ways. For this reason this book is divided into three sections: one for the girls, one for both sexes, and one for the boys.

In the girls section, you can find out about breasts and periods, sex hormones, and biology, as well as explore the feelings and issues that commonly concern girls.

In the section for both sexes, you can find out about the facts of life and issues that range from anorexia to acne. Everything in this section applies to both sexes.

In the boys section, you can find out about your voice breaking, erections, shaving, sex hormones, and biology, as well as explore the feelings and issues that commonly concern boys.

100% Girl

What makes

girls girls?

It's plain to see that girls are different from boys. So what makes girls girls? Girls' and boys' bodies are generally made up of the same stuff, but with four important differences.

① hormones

Estrogen (pronounced "es-trow-jin") is the female sex hormone that causes most of the changes during puberty. Progesterone, estrogen, and other hormones work together to control the menstrual cycle.

② sex organs

A girl's sex organs are inside her body, unlike a boy's. The brain and ovaries make female sex hormones, and the ovaries produce eggs. Tubes join the ovaries to the uterus. The vagina is a canal leading to the uterus. Women also have breasts that can produce milk.

The ovaries release an egg every month. If the egg is fertilized by a man's sperm, it will develop into a baby inside the uterus. If it is unfertilized, it leaves the body during menstruation (see pages 24 to 25).

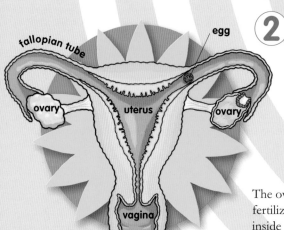

fallopian tube
egg
ovary
uterus
ovary
vagina

③ the brain

Scientists have long been interested in testing for differences between the brains of girls and boys.

There are physical differences between girls' and boys' brains. Girls' brains are smaller (although this has been proven to have no effect on intelligence—sorry boys!). During puberty, girls' brains also mature earlier than boys' brains do (although the boys catch up relatively quickly).

④ chromosomes

The sex chromosomes are one of the 23 pairs you have inside every cell in your body. Sex chromosomes are shaped like the letters X or Y. They determine whether you are a girl or a boy. You inherit one chromosome from each parent. If you have two Xs, then you're a girl. If you had an X and a Y, then you would be a boy.

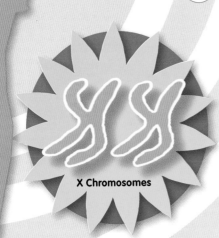

X Chromosomes

You have a pair of XX chromosomes in every body cell. That means every body cell—and there are more than 10 trillion of them—"knows" you are a girl!

Body talk

Our bodies change all the time throughout our lives. Women have four stages in their life cycle.

Our genes, strung together in strands of DNA inside every body cell, have a say in when we reach puberty or menopause.

2 Puberty

Puberty is when your body matures into an adult and you start your periods. It's a transition phase that leaves your body capable of having a baby.

1 Childhood

The first stage is childhood, from when you were born until the start of puberty.

Body shapes

Our bodies are all kinds of shapes and sizes. Yours is destined to be a certain body type—it's in your genes! Which one do you think is most like you?

The Hourglass
Curvy hips and bust and a narrow waist.

The Pear
Narrow shoulders, wide hips, thighs, and bottom.

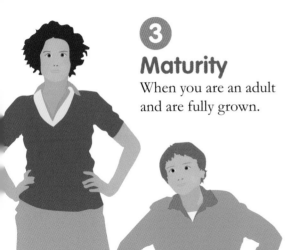

③ Maturity

When you are an adult and are fully grown.

④ Menopause

Menopause happens when a woman's periods stop and she can no longer have a baby.

Body put-down free zone

However you turn out, try not to be negative about your body. Who you are is FAR more important than what you look like. *Consider these points:*

>> Take average height–weight ratios with a grain of salt. Your correct weight is the one you're comfortable with and that allows you to live a happy, healthy, and active life.

>> We are bombarded with touched-up images of styled-up slim women in magazines, ads, everywhere! These can make us feel that they are normal, and we are not.

>> People can feel badly if they weigh above average, or even average. Or they may feel too thin. There aren't many winners in the game of comparison.

The Apple
Top heavy with a larger bust and tummy but thin legs.

The Tube Shape
Slender, fewer curves, like a typical model!

It all STARTS in your brain. ▼

THE HORMONE

What kick-starts puberty?

1 **A gene starts the ball rolling.**

The *pituitary gland* and the *ovaries* are hormone factories. They increase production during puberty and that not only changes your body, but can affect your mood, too.

2 It wakes up the HORMONES responsible for all the changes experienced during puberty. ▼

DID YOU KNOW?
Hormones are chemical messengers. They tell the cells in your body what to do when.

DID YOU KNOW?
Hormones can make you moody and tearful, and fill you with romantic feelings...

3 **There is no going back now!** ▼

DID YOU KNOW?
30 different hormones work in your body, regulating such things as your sleep, temperature, and hunger.

4 Let's meet the hormones... ▼

5 **GnRH hormone** is made in the pituitary gland at the base of your brain. This hormone works constantly throughout puberty. ▷

6 **Human growth hormone,** also made in the pituitary gland, does just what its name suggests—it makes you grow! ▷

7 **Estrogen** is the female sex hormone. It is made in the ovaries and causes most of the changes to your body during puberty. ▷

FACTORY

Follow the numbers around to find out.

16
average age 15½
adult breast size
usual age 12-19

15
average age 13
first period
usual age 10-16

WELCOME TO THE HORMONE FACTORY!

The pituitary gland sends hormones to the ovaries that make them come to life. Then the ovaries send hormones to the rest of the body, telling it to start changing.

brain

pituitary gland

ovaries

14
average age 13
underarm hair appears
usual age 10-16

13
average age 12½
hips widen, body gets curvier
usual age 8-15

12
average age 12¼
growth spurt peaks
usual age 8-14

Progesterone is also made in the ovaries and works with estrogen. Its job is to help control the menstrual cycle (periods).

9
Here's how your body changes...

10
average age 11¼
breasts start to grow
usual age 8-14

11
average age 11¾
pubic hair starts to appear
usual age 9-15

GIRL >> WOMAN

START HERE

Puberty can start anytime between the ages of 7 and 13. 10½ is the average age.

One sign that things are about to happen is that you start to grow taller more quickly.

The area around your nipples gets bigger and darker.

Your skin is oily and sweaty. You'll need to use deodorant.

Oh no! ZITS!!! You may get more pimples . . .

Romantic feelings!

Breasts grow some more. Take a look at them from the side.

Hormones surging!

Periods may bring PMS (Premenstrual syndrome), and make you feel rotten.

. . . especially before your period.

You are getting curvy now as your body fat moves to your hips, buttocks, and thighs.

Not all girls have hourglass figures—it depends on your genes. Some girls have big breasts, some have small, and some have medium!

Puberty can be *challenging*, so it's nice to know what to expect and when. Follow the *arrows* to learn the *stages of puberty*. Keep in mind that this is a general guide. Every body is different.

Your nipples become raised and your breasts start to grow.

A few long, downy hairs appear between your legs. These are your first pubic hairs.

A sprinkling of underarm hair appears, too. (This can come anytime—and over a period of months and years, rather than overnight.)

NEXT . . .

Peak growth time! You are growing like a weed!

Your period could start anytime now.

Maybe by 4 in (10 cm) in a year, or more!

Your breasts start to fill out.

You may find that you gain a little weight. This is normal and will disappear in the next stage . . .

Feel emotional? Get upset easily? Blame your hormones.

GOOD JOB...
you made it!

Now you can enjoy some of the good things about getting older.

Vrrroom!

Growing UP

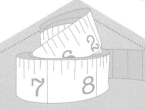

Puberty means you are *growing into an adult* and your body is changing into a *woman's*. But how is it growing? Which specific parts? And what will your body be like when it's finished?

Breast facts

• It takes on average two to three years for your breasts to bud.
• If you start puberty early, your breast growth may slow down and even stop for a few years while the breasts are still buds.
• When you gently squeeze your breasts between your thumb and index finger, if there is a half inch (1 cm) of tissue, it is likely that your breasts are starting to grow and puberty has begun.

Am I normal?

You may feel you are not growing quickly enough, or too quickly. You look in the mirror and think: "Am I normal?" The answer to that is no one is normal! Look around you—everyone is completely different.

Getting breasts

The first stage of puberty is an exciting one—your breasts start to grow! There are five stages of breast development (on a measure called the Tanner scale).

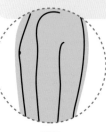

Stage 1
Before puberty—there is no breast tissue.

Stage 2
"Breast bud" stage—there is a small mound of breast tissue under the nipple, and the part around the nipple, called the areola, is starting to grow bigger.

Stage 3
The breast and areola grow bigger still—the nipple does not yet stick out.

Stage 4
The areola and nipple begin to stick out from the breast. (Some girls skip this stage.)

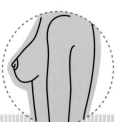

Stage 5
Breasts are fully grown. Now only the nipple sticks out. The areola is again level with the rest of the breast.

Getting hairier

Pubic hair (and underarm hair) can start growing even if puberty hasn't started yet. This is because their growth is not ruled by the puberty hormone estrogen, but by a different hormone. Here are the Tanner stages.

Stage 1
No pubic hair.

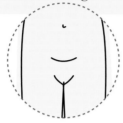

Stage 2
Sparse growth along the sides of the opening of the vagina. These dark hairs can be straight or slightly curled.

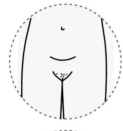

Stage 3
Hair is darker and curlier and now spreads thinly over the pubic area.

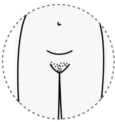

Stage 4
Hair is thicker and looks like an adult's, but covers a much smaller area.

Stage 5
Hair is adult in quantity and type and looks like an upside-down triangle.

Getting taller

Before puberty begins, you have been growing by about 2 in (5 cm) a year, but once it gets going, you shoot up—by about 4 in (10 cm) a year! In many girls, this happens sometime between ages 10 and 12, but it really varies. You may shoot past the boys, only to be overtaken two to three years later, when the boys have their growth spurts.

There's a good chance your body will look similar to either your mom's or dad's.

It's in your genes

We can't choose how we look—it was decided for us when we were created. Your parents passed on their genes and those genes helped to decide your size and shape, your eye color, even whether you have freckles or not. Your height is just one of your features decided by your genes.

The *breast* basics

You and your **breasts** are together for **life**. And puberty is when they make their appearance. **Big or small**, eagerly anticipated, or somewhat dreaded, breasts are two bumps on a person's body that **can seem like a very big deal.**

When do they start to grow?

Breasts can start growing at any age between 8 and 13, and everyone grows them at different rates. This can be tough if you are 11, your best friend is fully developed, and you're still flat-chested. Rest assured that nature will run its course and you will get your adult breasts eventually.

What are they for?

Your breasts are part of your reproductive system. They mean that someday if you have a baby your breasts will make the milk that your baby needs to survive.

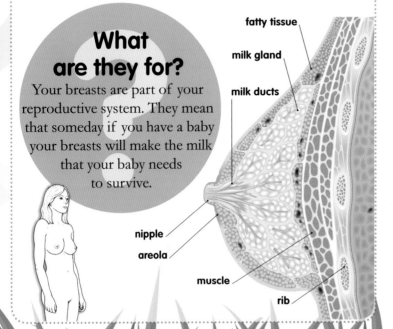

fatty tissue

milk gland

milk ducts

nipple

areola

muscle

rib

A girl's *breast friends*

You may love your new breasts, or you may barely notice them. But some women find fault with their breasts. Girls with big breasts may feel uncomfortable lying on their fronts, or jiggling as they run, while girls with smaller chests may feel less womanly. But, big or small, your breasts are part of you and the best way forward is to learn to love them.

Growing pains

Issue	Advice
One is growing faster than the other	Don't worry about this since they usually even out later. Even if you end up with one breast bigger than the other, this is completely normal, and you will be the only one to notice.
Your breasts feel sore and tender	This is perfectly normal and due to hormones. It can be especially noticeable before and during your period.
Your breasts feel lumpy	This is usually normal, but don't hesitate to talk to a doctor or school nurse if you are worried.
Unusually large breasts	If you feel your breasts are particularly large, you'll probably just grow into them. Occasionally though, this can be caused by a rare condition called "pubertal macromastia." Get checked out by a doctor if you are concerned.
Stretch marks	As your breasts grow you may see fine lines appearing on them. These will fade away with time.
Nipples that don't stick out	Teenagers often have flat nipples that will stick out later. An "inverted nipple" is when the nipple is tucked in to the breast. Boys can have these, too. This is just the way you are and lots of other women are the same (about 10%).
Hairy nipples	Long dark hairs around the nipple are very common in men and women. You can pluck or cut them if they bother you.

BRA shopping

Shopping for a bra can be *bewildering*. There are *many types* to choose from, and the *sizing isn't that straightforward*. It has been estimated that about 75–80% of women do not wear a properly fitting bra. So follow this guide to choosing a comfortable and correctly fitting bra—*it's an important skill for life*.

<< First bras

You may want to buy a bra when your chest starts to develop, or if you haven't started to develop but would like to wear a bra. First bras have flat or nearly flat cups and can be found in their own section in lingerie stores or department stores.

<< Soft-cup bras

These don't usually have underwires and are comfortable, but may not completely control any bounce or jiggling. They come in lots of different fabrics and thicknesses.

<< Underwire bras

These are not recommended as a first bra and need to be carefully fitted so the wires (which are sewn in along the lower edge and sides) don't dig in. However, a comfortable underwire bra lifts and holds breasts well and looks smooth under tops.

<< Sports bras

These are often a good first-bra option, too. They don't have traditional cups and are very comfy. Good sports bras provide excellent support and are often designed to keep you cool. For larger breasts, sports bras with molded cups work best.

fit tips

Breasts should not spill out of the sides or top. If they do, the cups are too small.

The cups should not wrinkle or pucker. If they do, the cups are too big.

The middle of the bra should sit on your chest.

The straps adjust to allow you to change the fit for each breast.

You should be able to slip two fingers under the band at the back. The band should be in the middle of your back (not pulling high or slipping low).

Many bra stores offer a free fitting service that is really worth taking advantage of. It's also good to know how to measure yourself. Here's how.

Measuring the BAND size >

You need a tape measure. *Wrap it* around your *rib cage* right *under your breasts*. Be sure the tape is even and not hiked up at the back. The tape should be snug, not tight. Take the measurement in inches rather than centimeters since bra sizes are always given in inches.

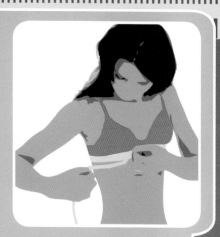

< Measuring the CUP size

Measure around your breasts at the *fullest part* (probably at the nipple level). If the *band* size is *larger* than the measurement around your nipples, your cup size is AAA. If the band size and the measurement around your nipples are the same, your cup size is AA.

If the band size is smaller than the cup measurement, *use this guide.* >

up to 1 in (2.5 cm) = A
up to 2 in (5 cm) = B
up to 3 in (8 cm) = C
up to 4 in (10 cm) = D
up to 5 in (13 cm) = DD
up to 6 in (15 cm) = E

Inside and out

Unlike a man's, a
woman's sex organs
are hard to see. So let's
take a look and find out
what they are all about.

on the outside...

This is your own body
and it is natural to want
to see what it looks
like. So take a look!
The best way to see
between your legs
is to grab a mirror
and follow this
guide to your vulva.

THE CLITORIS
This is a small mound
of skin the size of a
pea. It is the most
sensitive to touching
and sexual feelings.

URETHRA
A small opening through
which urine from the
bladder leaves the body.

LABIA
These are the flaps of skin
that cover the openings to the
vagina, urethra, and clitoris.

VAGINAL OPENING
This is the opening of the passageway
from the female sex organs to the
outside of the body. It is bigger than
the opening to the urethra.

female **SEX** *organs*

THE HYMEN
At the entrance to your vagina, you may see a thin
membrane of skin with one or more openings. This
is called a hymen. This is often broken during a girl's first
experience of sexual intercourse. But it can be torn or
stretched after an accident, or by exercise like gymnastics
or horseback riding without a girl even noticing.

What's a nana?

The female genitals have always been an awkward subject. Some people feel embarrassed to say "vagina." To combat this, society has come up with slang words.

on the inside...

A woman's sex organs lie inside her pelvis and are made up of two ovaries that connect to her uterus and vagina. The different parts all do different jobs.

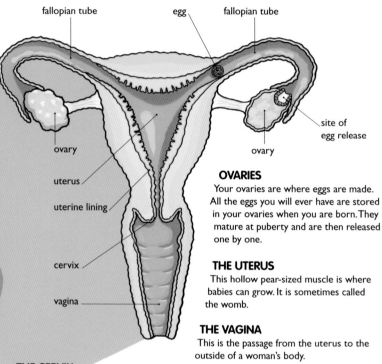

fallopian tube

egg

fallopian tube

site of egg release

ovary

uterus

uterine lining

cervix

vagina

ovary

OVARIES

Your ovaries are where eggs are made. All the eggs you will ever have are stored in your ovaries when you are born. They mature at puberty and are then released one by one.

THE UTERUS

This hollow pear-sized muscle is where babies can grow. It is sometimes called the womb.

THE VAGINA

This is the passage from the uterus to the outside of a woman's body.

THE CERVIX

The cervix is a small opening at the lower end of the uterus. It connects the uterus to the vagina and can open wide when a baby is born.

FALLOPIAN TUBES

Each tube is about 3 in (7.5 cm) long and the width of a drinking straw. The fallopian tubes connect the ovaries to the uterus.

Here are a few...
vajayjay
cha cha
hoo ha
lady business
flower
privates
goodies
nana
lala
po-po
toto
cho cho

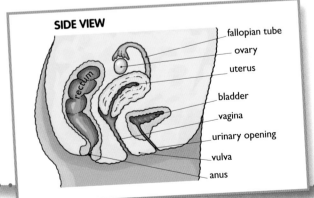

SIDE VIEW

rectum

fallopian tube

ovary

uterus

bladder

vagina

urinary opening

vulva

anus

MASTURBATION

This is the feeling or rubbing of genitals in a way that feels good. Masturbation is private and a perfectly normal thing to do. And despite what you may have heard, it can't harm you in any way.

The female cycle

In nature there are many cycles: that of the Moon, the seasons, the water cycle, and the menstrual cycle! That last one applies to us girls. Has yours started? No? From your mom to your girlfriends, everyone suddenly wants to know.

The science bit

As a woman releases an egg each month, the lining of her womb becomes thicker to prepare itself for pregnancy. If the egg is fertilized by a man's sperm, this lining will then gently cushion the egg as it develops into a baby. If the egg is not fertilized, both the egg and lining leave the woman's body through the vagina—and this is the bleeding you experience during your period.

What it means to you

This is the most dramatic step from girl to woman of the whole puberty process. It can make you feel excited, shocked, relieved (at last!), panicked, or a little of all that. The first thing most girls see in their underwear is NOT a great flow of redness. In fact, it is often just brownish red and very light to start with, giving you plenty of time to figure out clothing protection.

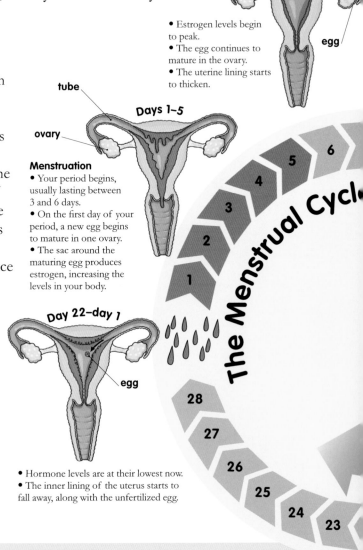

Days 6–12
- Estrogen levels begin to peak.
- The egg continues to mature in the ovary.
- The uterine lining starts to thicken.

egg

tube

Days 1–5

ovary

Menstruation
- Your period begins, usually lasting between 3 and 6 days.
- On the first day of your period, a new egg begins to mature in one ovary.
- The sac around the maturing egg produces estrogen, increasing the levels in your body.

Day 22–day 1

egg

- Hormone levels are at their lowest now.
- The inner lining of the uterus starts to fall away, along with the unfertilized egg.

The Menstrual Cycle

6
5
4
3
2
1
28
27
26
25
24
23

Period pain

There is hardly a woman on Earth who hasn't experienced period pain. The pain is caused by the womb contracting and shedding its lining (as a period) so a new lining can grow. There are ways to treat it. Exercise can ease the pain (though you might not feel like it), a hot-water bottle on your lower stomach may do the trick, and, if all else fails, taking painkillers (according to the enclosed instructions) should fix the problem. Severe pain should always be reported to a doctor.

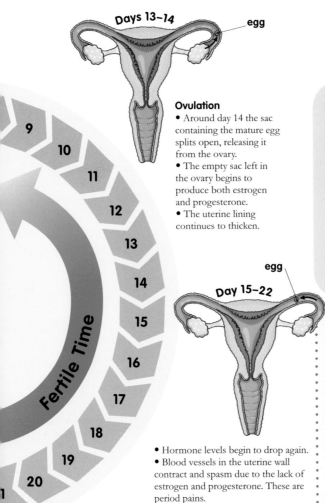

Days 13–14

egg

Ovulation
• Around day 14 the sac containing the mature egg splits open, releasing it from the ovary.
• The empty sac left in the ovary begins to produce both estrogen and progesterone.
• The uterine lining continues to thicken.

egg

Day 15–22

• Hormone levels begin to drop again.
• Blood vessels in the uterine wall contract and spasm due to the lack of estrogen and progesterone. These are period pains.

Fertile Time

9
10
11
12
13
14
15
16
17
18
19
20
1

PMS

PMS is short for premenstrual syndrome and is felt to some degree by three out of four women. It is caused by a hormone imbalance up to two weeks before your period and is not serious. However, it can give you food cravings, headaches, pimples, and sore breasts, and make you feel emotional and irritable. A healthy, balanced diet and regular exercise can help. So can diet changes. Ask your doctor if you suffer badly.

Things to know
• There can be much longer gaps between periods when you first start menstruating, and periods can be irregular.
• Women have different-length cycles. If your periods are regular, count the days between day 1 of your period, and day 1 of your next period to give you the length of yours.
• Though it may look like a lot, the average amount of blood is only about 2 tablespoons for an entire period.
• About 6 months or so before getting your first period, you might notice odorless, clear or white vaginal discharge.

In the BATHROOM

You may find you are spending *more time* in the bathroom—there is so much *more to do* there, what with zits, periods, and hairy legs! Your siblings may be banging on the door, but tell them to wait—what you are doing is important.

MAKEUP

When it comes to makeup, less is more! A dab of lip gloss, a sweep of blusher, and a wave of mascara should be enough to enhance your natural, fresh-faced beauty. For special occasions, you could add a little glitter into the mix. Painting your toenails is a fun way to experiment with color.

Top tips
Experiment with what works with your skin color. And remember to remove all your makeup before bedtime!

HAIR REMOVAL

Most of us buy our hair-removal products at the drugstore. These vary a lot. Depilatory (hair-removing) creams provide a pain-free option, but the results can be patchy and the creams are smelly! Shaving cream applied thickly to damp legs and armpits, then shaved with a razor is a fuss-free answer. Self-waxing can be painful (but the effects last longer—up to 4 weeks).

SHAVING

Always use a sharp razor, as a blunt one is not effective and can damage your skin. Don't share razors and always be extremely careful with them. Nicks can happen!

WAX

Always follow the manufacturer's instructions when using self-waxing kits.

PERIOD PRODUCTS

It's a good idea to keep some sanitary napkins handy in case you start your period. (If it starts at school and you don't have one, ask to visit the school nurse, who will be able to help you.) Girls generally begin by using sanitary napkins to catch menstrual blood. These can easily be secured to your underwear. When using tampons, wash your hands before and after their use and always read the manufacturer's instructions carefully before using any type of tampon.

When is the right time to start using tampons? Some people have specific ideas regarding this issue, but the general rule is—when you feel you want to.

tampons
Choose the slimmest available tampons when you are starting to use them and wait until the heavy part of your period to insert one. Try to relax. If you are tense it can make putting a tampon in more difficult.

sanitary napkins
These are an easy-to-use method for absorbing blood and work like a wad of absorbent cotton. You may think they are big and bulky and that everyone must notice your bulging crotch, but that is not the case. No one will notice them.

PERSONAL HYGIENE

After the start of puberty, you sweat more, and your skin produces more oil from oil glands. This can start to smell and produce body odor (B.O.). This is easily avoided by showering every day, especially after sports, and by using a good deodorant.

a white smile
You now have your adult teeth and need to take care of them. Brush your teeth at least twice a day and make sure to floss. This helps prevent tooth decay and bad breath.

sweet smelling
Deodorant allows you to sweat but prevents odors. Antiperspirant stops your sweat glands from sweating.

feet
Keep your feet clean and always wear socks with sneakers.

body sprays
Body sprays help mask any bad smells. They are a little like cheap perfumes. Remember not to spray on too much!

LOVE life

Puberty marks the start of you as a woman—and the beginning of your *love life*. You may begin to have **strong romantic feelings** early in adolescence, or you may experience none at all. Both are normal. One thing to keep in mind is that you are just at the beginning of your love life, and this will last for the rest of your life, so there is really **no hurry!**

Crushes

A crush is an intense, joyous feeling you get when you think about someone. You may get a crush on someone for a short time only, or a crush can be intense and long lasting. If you have a crush, you may dream about a relationship together and obsess over your crush. It can be magical, painful, and torturous. It's like a romantic hero-worship.

Type 1

Many young girls develop crushes on rock stars or movie stars, teachers, adults, friends' older brothers—the object of the crush is often out of reach. Crushes are a good way to rehearse romantic feelings, without having to act or what to say. Deep down, you know it is unlikely there will ever be a relationship.

Type 2

If you develop a crush on someone your own age, who you know, complications can creep in. Should you let him know? Does he like you back? If he does, this can be really exciting—or it can have the opposite effect! If you do decide to let him know, test the water first to see if he seems to like you, too. Just striking up a casual conversation with him is usually best… and make sure you do it in private. If his friends are there listening, he may act cool.

Don't be crushed by a crush!

You may experience the misery of having your feelings rejected. This is never a happy situation, and can make you even more attached than you were before. Here are a few tips to help you get over it:

1. **Confide** in your **friends** and ask them to distract you.
2. Throw yourself into your schoolwork and make sure you don't fall behind.
3. Take up a new *hobby*—something that gets you out of the house and gets you moving.
4. Allow yourself some time alone to fantasize about your crush, but *don't let it take over your life.*

Just good friends

After you reach a certain age and you are friends with a boy, it may attract unwanted attention—even if you have known him all your life! Even adults may gently tease you, and ask "Is he your boyfriend?" You can ignore this, or explain that you really are just good friends and there is nothing more to it!

Gay and straight

Sometimes girls develop crushes on other girls. This is normal, too, and doesn't necessarily mean you're gay. During puberty, and especially through the teen years, people explore and discover their sexuality.

Karen loves Sam

Heterosexual (straight) means being sexually attracted to the opposite sex. The majority of people are heterosexual.
Homosexual (gay or lesbian) means being sexually attracted to the same sex. It is estimated that one in ten adults is homosexual.
Bisexual means being sexually attracted to both sexes.

Having romantic feelings for other girls may make you feel confused, especially if you have heard insulting slang about it. Research has shown that nearly everyone at some point feels romantic about someone of the same sex. Finding out what your natural sexuality is can take time, or you may know for sure right away. Everyone is different. Being homosexual is not a choice. It is a part of who you are, the same as being heterosexual is part of who you are. Being homosexual is a perfectly healthy, normal, and acceptable way to be.

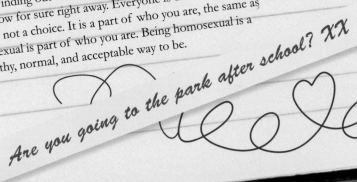

Are you going to the park after school? xx

Is it

True Love?

or just a crush

Q.1

How many times a day do you think about him?

A. Who? I like more than one person!

B. At least five times.

C. Pretty much every other second.

Q.2

You see him in the hall talking to another girl. How do you react?

A. I don't think anything of it.

B. Fine—it's really cool that he has friends who are girls.

C. Furious! Do those girls really think he's available?

Q.3

How long have you known him?

A. We haven't spoken to each other at all yet.

B. We have known each other for some time.

C. I don't know how we could talk! I am completely tongue-tied whenever he's around!

Mostly As: You are completely crushed out! You are crazy about him, but he may not know you (or he may be your best friend—even more awkward!). Watch out that it doesn't take over your life and get some advice if you feel like you need some!

Mostly Bs: You are one smitten kitten! You feel confident in your feelings, and how he feels about you. You're cool that you both have your own lives. When you're together, you are yourself with him. This could be love!

Your stomach flips over when you think about him, you can't stop scribbling his name in your diary, and you find it hard to concentrate. What's going on? Is this love, or just a crush...

Q.4

Does he feel the same about you?

A.
I don't know. Maybe, maybe not. No big deal.

B.
Yes. He's told me he does.

C.
No. I don't think he knows I exist.

Q.5

Your friends are always totally honest with you. What do they have to say about your guy?

A.
They all like him, too. It's pretty funny!

B.
They like him and think we are a good match.

C.
They wish I would stop talking about him and get back to the normal fun me.

Q.6

Have you ever questioned your feelings about him?

A.
I haven't gotten that far!

B.
Yes, I recognize all his faults and they have no effect on how I feel.

C.
Of course not! There is no need to question my undying love.

Mostly As: You are playing it cool. You are having fun, and don't have a serious crush—yet! One might develop, or any interest may peter out, as someone, or something else catches your eye.

What's the difference? Here it is in a nutshell—a crush is usually baseless and is for superficial reasons, like you think the guy is cute, or you think he's funny. True Love is mutual—you truly know each other and spend time with that so It feels perfect, like it was meant to be!

Keeping FIT

Exercise is an *important part of life*, almost as important as eating, drinking, and sleeping. And during puberty, your body is growing, your muscles are developing, and the strength you get now will help keep you healthy for the rest of your life.

Martial arts

Running

Yoga

Try a new sport

Your changing body may make some sports harder to do (ballet with big breasts may not be fun). So now is a good time to try new sports. Karate and martial arts, as well as self-defense classes, are great choices for young girls. So if you're terrible at tennis, and hate field hockey, try to find a sport you like. You can guarantee there is one.

Warming up

As you grow older, warming up before exercise becomes more and more important. A child is naturally flexible and stretchy, but, as you've probably noticed, adults aren't! Although you're not elderly yet, your bones are growing heavier and longer, so your muscles have more work to do, making them more prone to injury. So warm up first!

DON'T OVERDO IT!

Exercising too much can become a COMPULSION and is linked with eating disorders such as

ANOREXIA (see pages 44–45).

Here are some more good reasons to exercise

✳ Your heart and lungs experience a growth spurt, so you can handle more exercise.

✳ Exercise helps you achieve your best weight and prevents obesity.

✳ It strengthens your heart, increases your energy levels, and sends more oxygen to all parts of your body.

✳ It helps deposit calcium in your bones—especially important in your teens. This is when you are building up the bone mass that will be with you for life.

✳ Exercise helps with hormonal mood swings, and helps period pain, too!

✳ Getting into good exercising habits now can last for life, with immense benefits to your health as you age.

" *It's* gross! "

You feel tired and emotional, and how come one day you're popular, and the next you're not?

Periods can be inconvenient, to say the least. PMS, stomach cramps, let alone bloodstained underwear and sheets, you name it…

How you look has taken on a new importance—what happened to just liking you for who you are?

Zits, braces, glasses…

You may feel you're not developing quickly enough… or that you're developing too quickly.

Boys! (You love them—really!)

"It's great!"

There are chances to make new friends, try out new things, and generally have lots of fun…

It's exciting getting curves.

You can experiment with makeup and clothes—and express yourself more in the way you look.

More and more independence. Staying out later at night! Having your own money!

And at the end of it all you can go to college and drive a car and vote. Puberty is really gradual; it doesn't happen overnight. There's plenty of time to get used to it and to develop.

Dates and parties. Plus, you can watch more grown-up films.

Exploding the

Will exercises make my breasts bigger?

No, you can't add inches to your breasts by exercising. Breasts are largely milk glands and fat, and there's no exercise to grow those. But exercise can make your breasts sit higher on your chest because it builds up the muscles directly below the breasts.

If I sleep on my stomach will my breasts grow more slowly?

No. The eventual size and shape of your breasts is in your genes, as is the rate at which they grow—sleeping on your front cannot slow down their growth.

I'll grow breasts that are the same size as my mom's.

This is not necessarily the case. You could inherit the breasts of your father's mother, or your aunt. Also, a woman's breast size can change when she has children, or loses or puts on weight. Women need to be remeasured for a new bra throughout the different stages of their lives.

MYTHS

Can a tampon pop out?

A tampon cannot disappear into your body. Nor can it fall out. Your vaginal wall is a strong muscle and it holds the tampon in place as it expands inside you.

Does having your period mean you can't do physical activity?

No. While you have your period, you can do any activity. You do, however, need to wear a tampon for swimming.

Boys won't like me if I'm not gorgeous.

When it comes to attracting the opposite sex, it's more important to have healthy self-esteem than big breasts. No one is ever going to look like Barbie or the air-brushed models in magazines, so learn to love who you are. Boys may all seem to like one or two girls in your class, but that may be because those girls are superficially glamorous and admiring them helps the boys to fit in. If you're interesting and friendly, and you care about other people, you'll attract friends of both sexes.

Can breasts pop?

No. Breasts cannot pop because they are made of fat and glands.

100% Me

The facts of life

Puberty changes our bodies from child to adult, that much we know. But **WHY** do we need puberty? Why can't we just grow taller to become adults? The answer to this is simple—***babies!*** Before puberty we can't have babies, but afterward, we can.

The sperm and the egg

A girl can become pregnant after her first period. A period means she is producing eggs. A boy can make a girl pregnant from his first ejaculation. This means he is producing sperm. If an egg and a sperm join together, then a baby can start growing.

HOW DO THEY JOIN TOGETHER?

1. Halfway through a woman's monthly menstrual cycle (see pages 24–25), an egg cell is released from one of her ovaries. It moves slowly along the fallopian tube, toward the uterus.

2. During sexual intercourse a man ejaculates inside a woman's vagina. About two teaspoonfuls of semen, containing millions of tiny sperm cells, are left in the top of the vagina.

3. Sperm cells swim through the cervix, through the uterus, and along the fallopian tube. Only a few hundred make it to the egg.

4. If one sperm gets into the egg, they join together and fertilization has happened. A baby can now start to grow inside the woman's body.

A baby starts to grOW

The fertilized egg starts to divide and grow into a ball of cells, which moves down to the uterus (or womb). The ball of cells settles into the thick lining of the uterus and begins to grow into a baby. This is the start of pregnancy.

Happy birthday!

A baby takes nine months to grow. When it is ready, the uterus contracts in spasms and the baby's head pushes against the woman's cervix until it opens up (this is called labor). Then the baby travels down the vagina and out into the world.

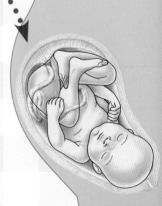

FOOD for thought

Eating healthily is always important, especially during puberty because you *grow* really fast during adolescence. Making a conscious effort to adopt *healthy eating* habits now will last you for life.

A healthy, balanced diet

Here is a guide to getting the right proportions of food in your diet. If every meal is balanced like this, you are doing well.

TIPS
- Eat fruit or vegetables for a snack—5 a day
- Use low-fat dairy products
- Watch your sugar intake
- Eat more oily fish
- Increase fiber in your diet
- Decrease the use of salt

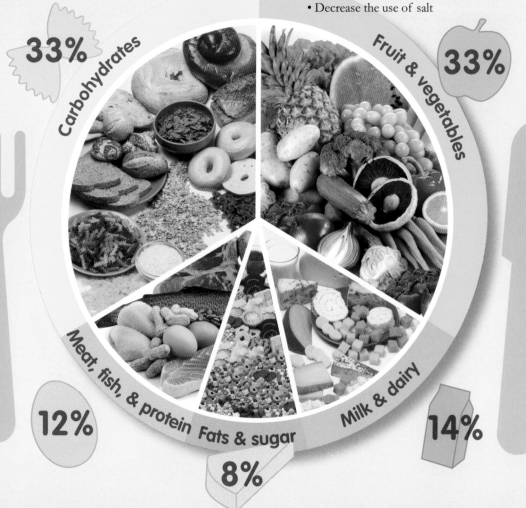

33% Carbohydrates

33% Fruit & vegetables

12% Meat, fish, & protein

Fats & sugar

8%

14% Milk & dairy

What kind of eater are you?

It's breakfast time. Do you...
A. Skip it, and spend extra time in bed.
B. Stuff a piece of toast in your mouth as you rush out the door.
C. Eat cereal and toast, or eggs and fruit, or a smoothie—you know, a healthy breakfast!

Sunday dinner. Do you...
A. Take a big helping of mashed potatoes, with gallons of gravy. Thanks, but no veggies!
B. Sample a little of everything and gobble it all down.
C. Have a small portion of potatoes, lots of veggies (your favorite!). Just a splash of gravy.

You feel the need for a snack. What do you choose?
A. A candy bar.
B. Bread, potato chips, whatever's around.
C. A piece of fruit, some seeds or nuts.

You are eating out at a diner with friends. What do you choose?
A. Burger and fries.
B. Whatever everyone else is having.
C. Chicken or fish with potatoes and veggies.

You're thirsty. What do you drink?
A. A sugary soft drink.
B. Soda or juice, or whatever you can find.
C. A glass of water, or a small glass of fruit juice to add to your 5-a-day.

Mostly Cs
You're a very healthy eater. The habits you have now will last you a lifetime—excellent!

Mostly Bs
You're a convenience eater. Whatever is available, you'll eat and you don't think much about it, so long as you're full! Try eating more fruit and veggies, and be conscious of your 5-a-day.

Mostly As
You're not a very healthy eater. Choose more vegetables, fruits, lean meats, and fish. You'll feel better, and good eating habits can last a lifetime.

Overweight?

Obesity—or being very overweight—is twice as common in adolescents today than it was 30 years ago. Obesity can lead to high blood pressure and type 2 diabetes. Most obese kids simply eat too much and exercise too little. Because of society's negative attitudes, many obese adolescents have a poor self-image and, therefore, might become less and less active, and then feel more and more alone.

To keep from being overweight try to:
• develop healthy eating habits
• exercise regularly
• not focus on losing a specific amount of weight

Counseling can help adolescents cope with their problems, including poor self-esteem. For help and advice contact your doctor.

the BODY

Too fat? Too thin? Too short? Too tall?
Your body is going through huge
changes, which can be both exciting
and frightening.

a cascade of changes

Change is scary and with all the hormones flowing through
your body you might start criticizing the way you look. You
might even start comparing your body to celebrities you see
in magazines and on TV. But do they have the perfect body
or the body impossible?

thin or false?

Celebrities parade for the camera. But, not everything is as it seems.
Photographs and even movies are often altered to make people look
better than they really do, not to mention all the money stars spend on
stylists! Being thin isn't the only way to be beautiful; we are all different
and unique, and remember—personality is a huge part of attractiveness.

eating disorders

When people become obsessed with their bodies and how
they think they look, they can develop an eating disorder.
This is when people try to change their body by using bad
eating habits. Eating disorders are especially dangerous during
puberty because your body is growing at a terrific rate and
needs nutrition. The eating disorder that most commonly
affects adolescents is called anorexia nervosa.

*We grow up with unrealistic images of
the human body, and this can make us
think we aren't shaping up to the ideal.*

IMPOSSIBLE

Eating disorders are normally associated with girls. However, new figures now show one in ten anorexia cases are boys.

anorexia

Anorexia is when someone severely limits his or her eating to lose weight. Here are the danger signs:

* losing lots of weight
* continuing to diet although thin
* feeling fat, even after losing weight
* feeling anxious about gaining weight
* fussy eating
* obsessing about food
* not eating with family or friends

what to do...

If you think you may have anorexia, it is very important to talk to your doctor immediately, or to a trusted adult. Even if it is scary to get help, your life may depend on it.

how to help a friend

This can be tricky. Often, people with eating disorders don't want to talk about their problems. Don't let this stop you. People with anorexia often need their friends or family to take the first steps to get help for them. Be patient with your friends and always offer a listening ear. Most importantly, tell a parent or teacher about your worries. Alternatively, you can contact the National Eating Disorders Association at 1-800-931-2237; this organization specializes in eating-disorder advice and support for individuals and families.

bulimia

People with this eating disorder go to extreme measures to control their weight. Sufferers secretly eat lots of food. These excessive moments are known as binge-eating. After binge-eating sufferers take laxatives or force themselves to vomit.

ZITS

Just when you least want one, you feel that tell-tale soreness, sense the brewing infection, and there it is—a zit! Pimples, zits, blemishes, acne, whatever you call them, they are a pain. Everyone hates them, but nearly everyone has to deal with them at some point.

Why now?

When puberty begins, the oil glands on your head, face, and body become more active. Excess oil can get trapped by a hair follicle so it can't empty out of the pores on your skin as it usually does. Instead, the oil builds up and forms a small plug in the pore that results in zits. They can appear anywhere, but usually show up on your face, neck, shoulders, and back.

Facts about acne

- Acne is most common among teenagers.
- 80% of all people between ages 11 and 30 have acne outbreaks at some point.
- Women develop acne earlier and are more likely to have it as adults.
- Men are ten times more likely to suffer from a severe form of acne.
- 40% of teens have acne that requires treatment from a doctor.
- Serious outbreaks can cause emotional and social problems—low self-confidence, as well as poor body image, and feelings of embarrassment, and frustration.
- No one can help having acne.

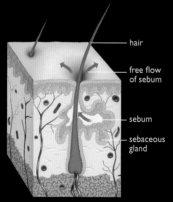

Normal hair follicle
Tiny open pores on your skin secrete an oily substance called sebum. Hormones can cause the skin to overproduce sebum.

Labels: hair, free flow of sebum, sebum, sebaceous gland

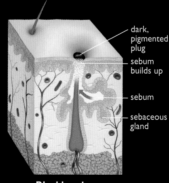

Blackhead
If the pore becomes blocked, a blackhead forms like a cap.

Labels: dark, pigmented plug, sebum builds up, sebum, sebaceous gland

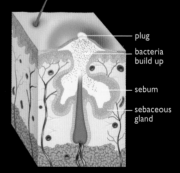

Infected follicle
Underneath, the trapped oil can breed bacteria. The area becomes inflamed and a zit appears.

Labels: plug, bacteria build up, sebum, sebaceous gland

The life and death of an annoying zit

"Mmmm! it feels nice and greasy here!"

A zit starts in a blocked oil gland.

"How to get a-head! Hee, hee, hee!"

Bacteria buildup at the site makes a painful red bump.

"Ugh! I keep getting attacked!"

Cells in your blood rush to fight the infection, producing white pus.

"I'll be back!"

That, combined with soap and some zit cream, help kill the zit.

How to fight back

Different cures work for different people. From over-the-counter acne creams, to natural remedies like tea-tree oil, to antibiotic lotions and prescriptions from the doctor, it's a case of finding what works for you.

General rules:

- Wash your face with warm water twice a day.
- Don't overdo it with harsh soaps and cleansers.
- Some sunlight on your skin is good for you (but never burn).
- Keep dirty hands off!
- If you must squeeze a zit, wash your hands first and stop once the pus is out. Squeezing out blood or clear fluid damages your skin. Afterward, dab with a mild antiseptic. Do not squeeze a red zit.
- If you get persistent acne and it's affecting your life, see a doctor.

ZIT MYTHS

Can you *spot* the true statements among these acne myths?

1. Eating chocolate and fries causes zits.
2. Having a dirty face means you get pimples.
3. Raging hormones before a menstrual period can make acne worse.
4. A little sun makes zits better.
5. Squeezing, popping, or picking zits will make them go away.
6. Pressure from sports helmets or equipment, backpacks, tight collars, or tight sports uniforms can cause zits.
7. Using heavy, greasy skin-care products can cause acne.

ANSWER: numbers 3, 4, 6, and 7 are true.

Tea tree oil

Zit cream

It's a *jungle*

School relationships can sometimes seem like they are straight out of a nature documentary. Read these common adolescent traits, and *see if you recognize any of them going on in YOUR school.*

Here's an experiment that was conducted on teens: teens took control in a driving simulation.

Players are encouraged to drive as far as they can in a fixed amount of time. Along the way, each player comes across eight traffic lights that turn yellow as the intersection is approached.

Lions

It's completely natural for some children to take the lead in school activities. Every prehistoric tribe, like every pack of lions, needed a leader in order to work successfully. That remains true for people today, and leadership qualities often show up during puberty.

Sheep

If there are leaders, there have to be followers, and, like sheep, many people don't like to stand out in the crowd. After all, it's always the leader who gets blamed for anything that goes wrong. Through puberty you may find you want to look and behave more like your friends than ever before, which isn't always a baaaaad thing.

Monkeys

People like to stay in groups for the same reason monkeys go around in troops. It gives us a sense of belonging and provides protection. Even though we don't need to protect ourselves from wild animals anymore, being part of a group still makes us feel safer and happier. As we hit puberty this feeling intensifies.

Peacocks

Just like the peacock showing off its beautiful plumage, some kids have all the gear. Human beings have always used objects to show how powerful or important they are. While our cavemen ancestors may have counted their sheep, today's children like to show off the latest sneakers or mp3 players.

Chameleons

Some kids are real chameleons—they change their look, friends, and style, and get along with everyone. These kids are usually friendly and fun. They make great friends, but don't expect to have them to yourself.

The player is faced with a dilemma: stop, and waste time, or go and risk crashing. When adolescents play the game, they take twice as many chances if their peers are in the room than if they are by themselves. No such peer effect is seen among adults.

I wanted to be accepted and be part of the group. This is a very important aspect of being human—it's a powerful feeling to an adolescent like me.

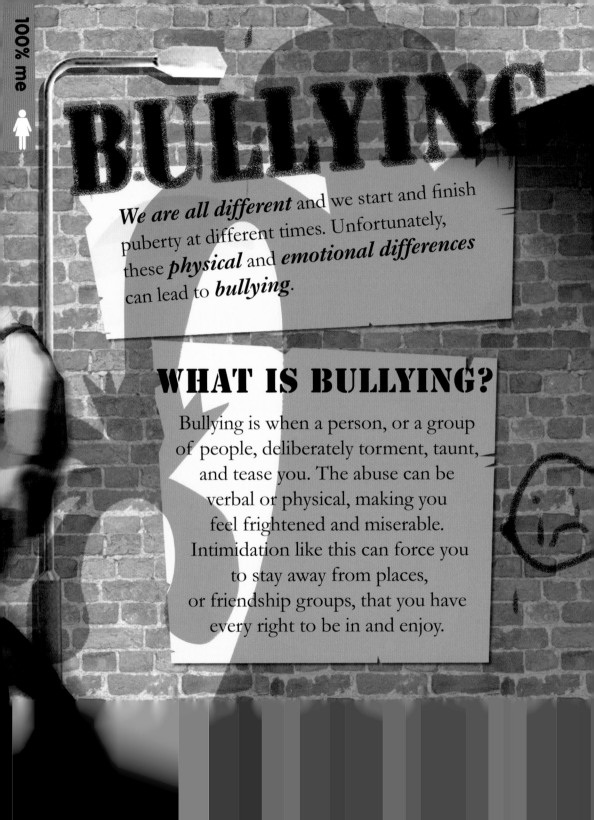

BULLYING

We are all different and we start and finish puberty at different times. Unfortunately, these *physical* and *emotional differences* can lead to *bullying*.

WHAT IS BULLYING?

Bullying is when a person, or a group of people, deliberately torment, taunt, and tease you. The abuse can be verbal or physical, making you feel frightened and miserable. Intimidation like this can force you to stay away from places, or friendship groups, that you have every right to be in and enjoy.

WHAT MAKES A BULLY?

There are many reasons why people bully. Most of the time bullies have their own problems and many have been bullied themselves. Also, a lack of understanding about what the body is going through and how to deal with it can lead to bullying. Bullies use differences, whether they are physical, racial, or sexual, to gain the upper hand. Sometimes, these differences can be as petty as being new to a town or school. The smallest thing can give a bully ammunition and encourage him or her to show off in front of a group. People who encourage bullies are bullies themselves.

TYPES OF BULLYING

- **PHYSICAL** – From punching and kicking to the physical damage or theft of a victim's belongings.
- **VERBAL** – Name-calling can be deeply hurtful and is common in all aspects of bullying.
- **SEXUAL** – Touching, insinuating, and pressuring the victim to perform or endure acts they don't understand or enjoy.
- **CYBER** – Harassment using email, texting, and instant messaging has become a powerful weapon for bullies to invade a victim's private space, meaning they can bully 24/7 no matter where their victim is.
- **REJECTION** – Ignoring and pushing victims out of friendship groups, clubs, or activities can be used by groups of bullies to victimize and alienate.

HOW TO DEAL WITH IT
Don't suffer in silence... TELL, TELL!

Check out your school's antibullying policy and act on what you discover.

Don't feel ashamed. Tell your parents or teacher. They are there to help and support you.

Bullying is unacceptable, period. If you know it is going on, tell someone in authority. You can stay anonymous if you want to.

Need more information?
Visit the Department of Health and Human Services site:
www.stopbullyingnow. hrsa.org

GROUPS VS. GANGS

Friendship is a great relief during puberty. Realizing everyone is in the same boat can build and strengthen relationships. However, puberty can also be a time of pressure, especially from peers. Make sure your friendships are with the right people.

GROUPS

FRIENDSHIP GROUPS are normally formed around a mutual interest, like sports, movies, music, or just because you all like one another. This similar outlook brings together like-minded people who enjoy each other's company.

Being a member of a group allows you to have fun with friends, as well as create your own individual identity.

GOOD FRIENDS are...
Loyal
Trustworthy
Honest
Supportive
Good listeners

GANGS

GANGS, on the other hand, aren't all that they may seem. They share similar traits to friendship groups, although instead of promoting the individual, GANGS promote a mimic mentality and you can be forced to put the GANG's reputation before your own or your friends'. This can lead to trouble, especially during puberty, when understanding and finding yourself is so important.

BAD FRIENDS are...
Sneaky
Manipulative
Selfish
Pressurizing
Critical

...urself doing stuff that makes you feel uncomfortable or you don't want to do—SAY NO.

I JUST FELT LIKE IT!

If the only reason you can think of for particularly risky behavior is that you **just felt like it**, then you may be able to **blame** it on your **brain**. After all, you could say, your **basal ganglia**, the part of your brain that helps your **frontal cortex** (in charge of logical thinking) is not fully developed yet!

SCIENTISTS noticed some differences between the sexes. Girls' and boys' brains develop at different rates.

Amygdala grows faster in teen boys—this is responsible for gut reaction and **emotion**.

Cerebellum is 14% larger in boys—this is important for **physical coordination**.

The hippocampus, crucial for many **memory tasks**, grows faster in girls.

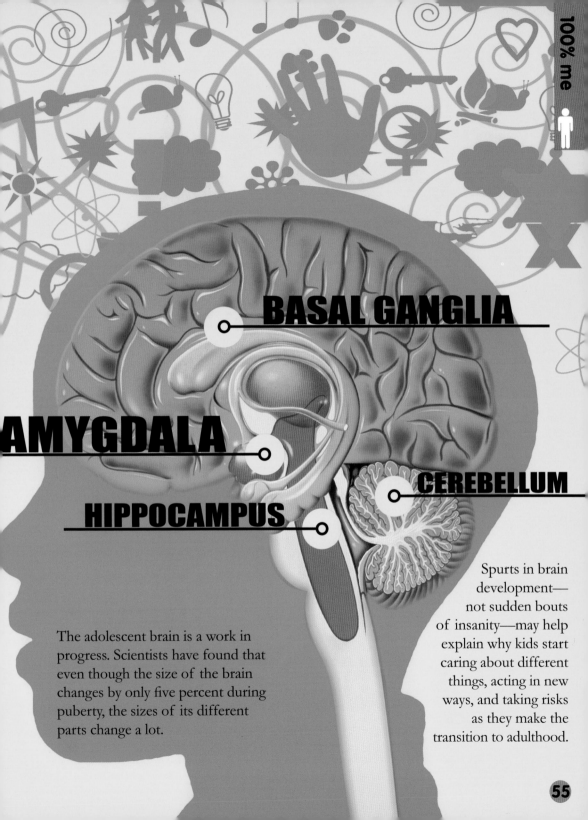

BASAL GANGLIA

AMYGDALA

CEREBELLUM

HIPPOCAMPUS

The adolescent brain is a work in progress. Scientists have found that even though the size of the brain changes by only five percent during puberty, the sizes of its different parts change a lot.

Spurts in brain development— not sudden bouts of insanity—may help explain why kids start caring about different things, acting in new ways, and taking risks as they make the transition to adulthood.

55

LEAVE

KEEP OUT

As you reach puberty, you may find that your parents start *bugging you*—even more than usual! *What's going on?* You are turning into an **adult**, and leaving your role of child behind.

This can put strain on the child/parent relationship, as you naturally want to stretch the bonds. It is all a necessary part of growing up, and most parents understand this and give new privileges. However, sometimes conflict can result.

COMMON CAUSES OF FIGHTS WITH YOUR FOLKS!

**!*?!?*
They make you go on family trips with them, when you'd rather be with your friends.

You want to go to the festival in the park. All your friends are going. Your parents say NO!

You want your ears pierced/hair dyed. Your parents object.

Your parents limit your computer use or won't let you watch certain TV shows.

Your parents don't like a new set of friends you've made.

In fact, this list could go on forever, and sometimes life at home can feel a little like a tug of war, especially as you hit the teen years.

ME ALONE!

Take these points into consideration

- Your parents love you and want the best for you. They are not trying to ruin your life!
- Parents worry about their children, sometimes too much, but it comes from the heart.
- Parents need to adapt to you turning into an adult, too. They may find it hard to let go of their baby.
- Parents have house rules, and, just because you are growing up, it doesn't mean those rules go out the window.

What can we do about it?

- COMPROMISE and BARGAINING—it's always worth a try!
- Being TRUSTWORTHY is a major winner with the folks. If you can prove that they can trust you again and again, you'll be allowed to do more.
- Always let them know WHERE you are, WHO you're with, what TIME you'll be back, and keep to it. You don't have to tell them every detail, but giving them some info will keep them from worrying.

DO NOT ENTER

WORLDS APART?

I like your shoes. Where did you get them?

From Shooz at the mall. They have them in blue and red, too! By the way, while I was shopping I saw Trudie. Remember her? She said she is still friends with Suzy Wagner!

Girls' talk?

Girls tend to talk about other people. They tell each other secrets, discuss school, and talk about things they want and need. They may also like talking about boys and clothes. Girls communicate using words and are good at talking about feelings.

Girls think boys...

... are immature (try having a serious talk with one!).
... show off and use bad language to try to act cool.
... think they are superstrong (all brawn, no brain!).
... pull stupid pranks and goof around.

But boys can also be...

... courteous, helpful, thoughtful, and kind.

Try not to judge the opposite sex, or lump them together.

Men and women often find it hard to understand each other. In fact, some say it's as though they come from different planets. But are **BOYS** really show-offs? And are *girls* catty? It's easy to generalize, but much better to look at people as individuals.

> Check out my mp3 player. It's the new classic with 160 gig storage. That's like 40,000 songs. And it plays videos!

> Cool. Did you see the game on Sunday? I went with my dad, and it was awesome. Our team was on fire and just kept scoring. It kind of reminded me of myself when I play!

BOYS'
talk?

Boys talk about things and activities—sports, mechanics, and how and why things work. Boys express their emotions through actions rather than words. They may lash out if they're angry, or withdraw to be silent and alone if they're hurt or upset.

Boys think girls…

… are mean, nasty, and always ganging up on each other.
… are shopaholics and always talking about shopping, sales, clothes, accessories, shoes, and jewelry…
… are scaredy cats—scared of the dark, storms, spiders…
… are capricious—always changing their minds.
… never stop talking—about nothing much!

But girls can also be…

… loyal, reserved, honest, and brave.

Everyone is an individual with a mixture of qualities.

100% BOY

What makes BOYS boys?

BOYS and GIRLS are different—it's a fact of life. So, what's going on under your skin that makes you a boy? Boys and girls are almost exactly the same, but with four important differences...

1 hormones

Testosterone! This powerful sex hormone is what makes boys boys. It has always been flowing around your body. But between the ages of 11 and 14 there is a huge rise in testosterone levels. This increase helps kick-start puberty and affects how you think, grow, and behave.

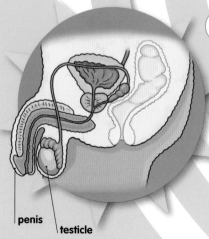

penis   testicle

2 sex organs

The male sex organs hang outside the body. They are the penis and the two testicles (the testes). When hormones trigger puberty, the testes begin to produce sperm and extra testosterone.

Every day a man makes between 50 and 500 million sperm in his testes, and the sperm take 1 to 3 weeks to mature.

③ the brain

Scientists have long been interested in testing for differences between the brains of boys and girls.

There are several physical differences between boys' and girls' brains. Boys' brains are bigger than girls' brains—unfortunately, that doesn't make boys more intelligent. Also, boys' brains mature more slowly than girls', but catch up eventually. A boy's brain is also good at judging distance and size, as well as making mental maps.

④ chromosomes

The sex chromosomes are one of the 23 pairs you have inside every cell in your body. Sex chromosomes are shaped like the letters X or Y. They determine whether you are a boy or a girl. You inherit one chromosome from each parent. If you have an X and a Y, then you're a boy. If you have two Xs, then you would be a girl.

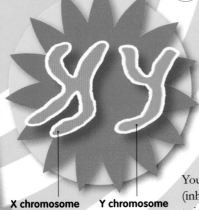

X chromosome **Y chromosome**

Your chromosomes are made of DNA and carry genetic (inherited) instructions that make you you. You have a pair of XY chromosomes in every body cell. That means every single body cell "knows" you're a boy. Man, that's a lot of cells in the know—more than 10 trillion!

63

Boys' bodies

Our bodies change all the time—that's part of growing up and getting old. Men have three main phases in their life cycle.

1 Childhood

This fun-filled phase starts at birth and ends when puberty and adolescence begin.

2 Puberty

The transition phase from childhood into adulthood. Your body and feelings change dramatically as you become capable of fathering a child.

Body types

During puberty your body changes shape and size. How it changes comes down to your genes, the amount of tissue types, and the levels of chemicals, like hormones, in your body.

REMEMBER These body types are general categories. See them as extreme points on a triangle—depending on your genes, you may be a mixture of the three.

ENDO MAN

ENDOMORPHIC (Apple body)

This body type has a wider waist and a large bone structure. An increase in fat-cell production gives a fuller figure, especially on the top half of the body.

3 Adulthood

You are now fully grown and have responsibilities—though don't forget to have fun!

Unlike the female body, the male body **DOESN'T** go through a menopause **stage.** Fertility does DECREASE as the body ages, although men can be fertile well into old age.

Keep going men, nearly there.....

Les Colley of Australia was **92** when he fathered his *ninth* child!

A GROWING CONCERN

One thing men have to endure, which most women don't, is baldness. Like so much stuff with your body, this is connected to your genes. It can start at any age, including your teenage years. It's hard to cope with, but remember, there is little you can do about it and it only affects how you look—it's not an illness or a disability.

MESO MAN

MESOMORPHIC (Rectangle body)

This is a more beefy body type with more muscle growth. Larger bones and low fat levels combine with wide shoulders to give a stocky appearance.

ECTO MAN

ECTOMORPHIC (Banana body)

This is a slim body type. Arms and legs are long, with a short upper body and narrow shoulders.

TESTOSTERONE

Testosterone is the main male *sex hormone* that helps kick-start puberty. It is produced in the testes and triggers sperm production, as well as prompting your *body to grow* and change. Testosterone doesn't just affect how you look on the outside—it also alters your *emotions* and how you feel on the inside.

Increased aggression

The huge surge in testosterone levels (800% more than when you were a toddler) during puberty can have some side effects. While it helps make you fit and strong, and can even help your emotional well-being, it can also make you become more angry and aggressive. It also triggers body hair and muscle growth, as well as making your voice break.

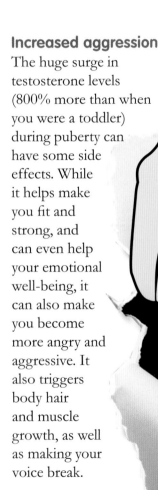

I think therefore I am... moody!

Hormonal upheaval can trigger emotional upheaval. You may become more self-conscious and experience *mood swings*. Many boys cry a lot more during early puberty. Don't worry. It's *perfectly normal*.

Feeling sexy?

As testosterone levels rise you will also begin to *produce more sperm* in your testes. This makes you have more *sexual feelings.* These feelings are new and they may take some getting used to. It's worth bearing in mind that although testosterone can make you feel different in lots of different ways, you don't have to act on any new feelings you may have.

The PREHISTORIC TIMES

THE CAVE ART OF HOW TESTOSTERONE HELPED MAN **SURVIVE**

A long time ago... (before yesterday)

Price—1 boar

GRRRR!

Testosterone gives me the strength and aggression I need for hunting wild animals.

LATER ON

I need good spatial awareness and physical coordination to be good at hunting (more effects of testosterone). One of these boar will feed my family for a week.

then...after a bit more time!

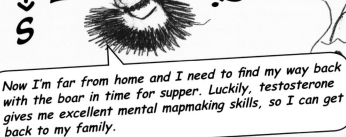

Now I'm far from home and I need to find my way back with the boar in time for supper. Luckily, testosterone gives me excellent mental mapmaking skills, so I can get back to my family.

NEXT WEEK... EVEN MORE AGGRESSION

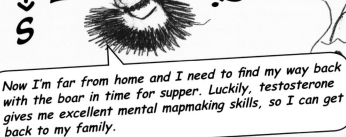

START HERE

The first signs of puberty are enlarged testicles and red scrotum, lengthening of the penis, and the growth of pubic hair.

Puberty can start anytime between 9 and 14. The average age is 11.

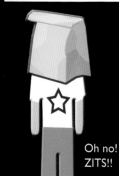

Oh no! ZITS!!

Your skin is oily and sweaty so you'll need deodorant and have to shower every day.

Testosterone surge! You have 800% more coursing around your body than when you were a toddler.

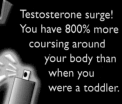

Two years after the start of puberty, boys hit a growth spurt. (Although not all boys are tall...)

More fights at school? Testosterone is taking over.

Some boys get really muscled; don't worry if you don't, since everyone's different.

Body hair—everywhere!

By midteens, you may need to start shaving.

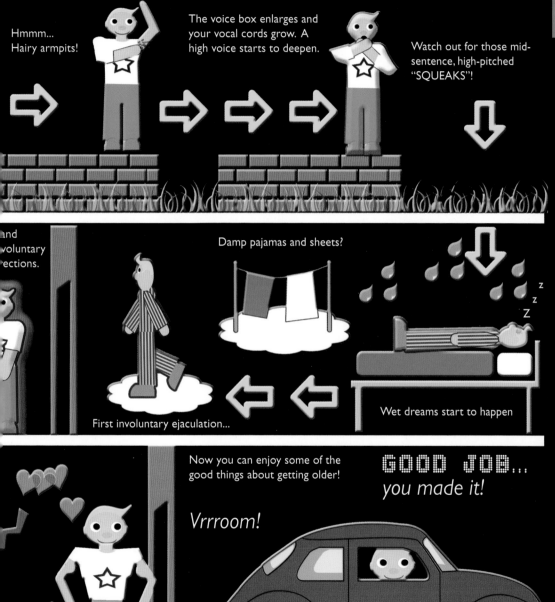

Puberty can be a *challenge*, so it's good to know what to expect, when. Follow the *arrows* to learn the *stages*. (Keep in mind that this is a general guide. Every body is different.)

Hmmm... Hairy armpits!

The voice box enlarges and your vocal cords grow. A high voice starts to deepen.

Watch out for those mid-sentence, high-pitched "SQUEAKS"!

...and ...voluntary ...rections.

Damp pajamas and sheets?

First involuntary ejaculation...

Wet dreams start to happen

Now you can enjoy some of the good things about getting older!

GOOD JOB... *you made it!*

Vrrroom!

...ong sexual urges... ...t's normal.

Outside and in

The **_male sex organs_** are mainly on the outside of the body. Because of this their **_change_** and **_growth_** are very noticeable. Let's take a quick look **_outside_** and **_in_** at what they are all about and what to expect during puberty.

on the outside...

Male sex organs all look different. Here's a general look at what's hanging where and why.

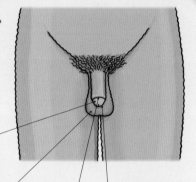

PENIS HEAD/TIP (Glans penis)
This is the most sensitive part of the penis. It's this area, once stimulated, that leads to ejaculation. There is an opening on the penis tip, called the meatus, where urine and semen exit the body.

SCROTUM
This pouch of skin hangs below the penis and contains and protects the testes.

FORESKIN
This sensitive layer of skin covers and protects the tip of the penis.

FRENULUM
This is the thin piece of tissue that connects the foreskin to the penis tip.

WHAT HAPPENED TO MY FORESKIN?
Not everyone has a foreskin. This is because at birth, or even as adults, you can have it removed. This is called circumcision and is done for religious, medical, or cultural reasons. Whether circumcised or not, the penis acts in the same way.

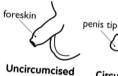

foreskin

penis tip

Uncircumcised penis

Circumcised penis

STAGES OF GROWTH

The appearance of your sex organs changes a lot during puberty.

1 PRE-PUBERTY
The penis grows with the rest of your body. It's small and only has one purpose—peeing.

2 EARLY YEARS OF PUBERTY
The testes start to grow. The scrotum skin thins and becomes darker and wrinkly.

3 MID-PUBERTY
The penis will start to lengthen. Pubic hair begins to grow.

4 LATE PUBERTY
The penis becomes wider and the tip more prominent. Pubic hair darkens, thickens, and becomes curly.

5 POST PUBERTY
Growth is complete.

on the inside...

It's easy to see and feel what's happening on the outside. But what's going on under the skin—how's it all connected? Here's an insight into the inside...

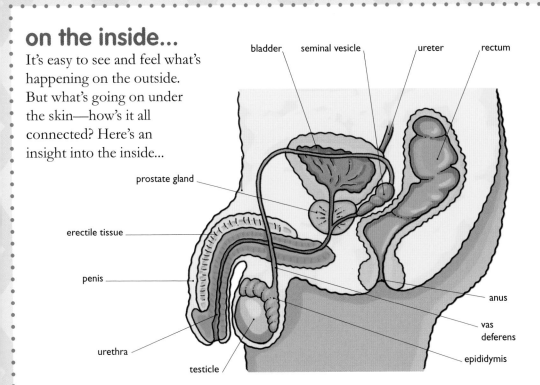

bladder   seminal vesicle   ureter   rectum

prostate gland

erectile tissue

penis

anus

vas deferens

epididymis

urethra

testicle

TESTES (testicles)
These are men's sexual factories. They produce the male sex cells (sperm), as well as the sex hormone testosterone.

URETHRA
This tube connects the bladder to the tip of the penis. It allows urine to exit the body. It is also used as a passageway for semen. When this happens, access from the bladder is cut off, allowing the semen to travel up and out of the penis.

EPIDIDYMIS AND THE VAS DEFERENS
Both testicles are capped by an epididymis. This is a small tubelike structure where sperm mature and get ready for their journey. Each vas deferens is a flexible tube up to 12 in (30 cm) long, that connects the epididymis to the urethra.

PROSTATE GLAND AND THE SEMINAL VESICLES
These glands produce the milky fluid that mixes with the sperm to create semen. Being suspended in the fluid allows the sperm to flow easily along their journey.

SEMEN
Approximately 70% of semen is fluid from the seminal vesicles, and 25% is fluid from the prostate. Only 5% of semen is sperm.

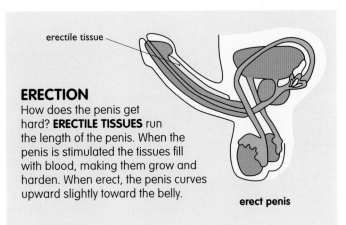

erectile tissue

ERECTION
How does the penis get hard? **ERECTILE TISSUES** run the length of the penis. When the penis is stimulated the tissues fill with blood, making them grow and harden. When erect, the penis curves upward slightly toward the belly.

erect penis

Living with "Willy"

Having a penis isn't always smooth sailing. There are many hidden quirks and annoyances waiting to happen, especially during puberty. Here's a rundown of what to expect from your penis.

Standing to attention

One thing that becomes more prominent during puberty is the erection. What's its purpose? It's all linked to reproduction. But you guys are all too young for that, so let's have a look at why it's happening now and why you can't always control it.

What is happening

An erection is a little like blowing up a balloon. Instead of air, it's blood filling erectile tissues that's making the soft penis harden and grow.

When and why?

To start with, erections can be hard to control—it happens to everyone. Here are a few examples of when your penis can stand to attention:

- when you are nervous or excited.
- when you need to urinate.
- while sleeping.
- and for no reason whatsoever!

Coping with erections

One of the more embarrassing erections you will face is the spontaneous kind. These happen for no reason—it's just your body getting used to the new sex hormones. Here are a few handy hints to help you deal with them:

- baggy clothes can conceal them.
- sit down to hide it.
- shield it with a bag or book.
- think about something else until it goes away.

Sperm factory

Your body will start to produce sperm at a terrific rate, on average 1,500 sperm every second, per testicle—that's nearly 260 million every day! This persistent buildup leaves the living space in your testes very cramped, so your body needs to release the excess sperm. This is achieved by ejaculation.

Wet dreams and masturbation

Boys will usually experience their first ejaculation between the ages of 11 and 15. Ejaculation is the release of semen, which contains sperm. A ***wet dream*** is when ejaculation occurs involuntarily during sleep. ***Masturbation*** is the rubbing of genitals in a way that feels good. Masturbation is private and perfectly normal. And despite what you may have heard, it can't harm you in any way.

SIZING UP

Size doesn't matter. There are only average statistics
out there about penis size, and averages never paint
the true picture. Basically, you are the size you are
supposed to be. The penis's main role is for
reproduction, and the vagina fits around it no
matter its shape or size.

What's a willy?

The male genitals have always been an
awkward conversational subject and some
people find it hard to say "penis." So, here
are a few alternatives.

HELLO
my name is

Willy

penis (general)
manhood
sausage
member
trouser snake
weiner
Johnson
tool
willy
wee-wee
dinkle

erect penis
woody
boner
chubby
hard-on

testicles
balls
nuts
cojones

**penis
and tesicles**
package
privates
family jewels

BODY HAIR
EVERYWHERE

The prospect of growing so much hair can be scary. But **don't worry**, you won't turn into a hairy monster every full Moon! Your body hair **will sprout gradually**. Here's a general guide to when and where to expect your hairy transformation.

From boy to man

When it comes to hairiness it's all in your genes. You often take after your parents. So, check out dad to see how hairy you might be.

Body hair—why it's there

Body hair is there for a reason. It traps dirt and germs and helps to keep you clean. Body hair also keeps you warm and protects sensitive areas, like your underarms and genitals.

facial hair usually starts to appear from 14 to 18 years old, although it can start earlier or later. The thickness, coverage, and color depends on your genes and can change throughout your life. Some men grow full beards, others just moustaches or sideburns.

Fact
An average adult male has about 5,000,000 hair follicles all over his body.

chest hair usually comes toward the end of puberty. Not all men grow chest hair, although you usually get a little growth around the nipples, even if you are not very hairy.

underarm hair develops between the ages of 11 and 13. This is a good sign that you should start washing under your arms every day and using deodorant.

arm and leg hair will start to grow darker and coarser. On your legs this will usually start from the pubic region down on to your thighs. Your shins and forearms will also show signs of thicker and darker hair growth.

pubic hair is the first area where hair growth usually starts. At around 11 to 13 years old, light and soft hairs will start to grow around the base of your penis. These pubic hairs will grow thicker, coarser, and curlier over time.

in the BATHROOM

CLEAN MACHINE

When you're exercising you sweat more, and even emotions like feeling nervous before a test can make your hands and neck feel clammy. You have millions of sweat glands all over your body. During puberty they become more active. More sweat means BODY ODOR! It's not the sweat that smells but the bacteria in it. So how do you stop the stink?

DAILY DOSE

The best way to beat B.O. is to wash every day. Bathing and showering with a good gel or soap will wash away the bacteria and keep you fresh and clean. Your genitals and underarms are important areas to target.

ANTIPERSPIRANT

Another way to avoid B.O. is to reduce the amount you sweat in the first place. Antiperspirant in a spray or roll-on keeps you drier.

DEODORANTS

Deodorants and body sprays work differently. They only mask the smell. These are better for people who don't sweat as much and can be a good place to start when puberty begins.

STEP UP

Much-forgotten smell villains are your feet. Sweaty feet are a perfect breeding ground for bacteria. Always remember to wash your feet after long walks and exercise.

SWEAT

Odor-eaters for your shoes may be helpful to mask any brewing smells.

You can also get **SPECIAL FOOT** deodorants to keep your feet dry.

ALSO, WEAR SOCKS!

THEY ABSORB THE SMELL, SO YOUR SHOES WON'T STINK. JUST REMEMBER TO CHANGE YOUR SOCKS EVERY DAY.

There is going to be far more to do in the bathroom: shaving, washing, and dealing with zits. Here are a few guidelines to help you cope with your changing body and keep you smelling and looking good.

A CLOSE SHAVE

Shaving for the first time can be scary, but it is also exciting. Here are a few hints and tips to help you master the art of shaving. First, there's a choice to be made: ELECTRIC or WET?

ELECTRIC

This is a good starting-out option. It is also quicker and there is less chance of cuts and nicks. However, it doesn't give as close a shave. The best tip is not to force the shaver into your skin, since this can cause irritation.

Never loan or borrow a razor—you can pass on or get infections!

WET SHAVE

For this you'll need a razor, either a disposable or one with a replaceable blade. Make sure the blade is sharp and clean. Shaving cream or gel allows the razor to glide across the skin and prevents soreness. Warm water will soften your hairs and make them easier to cut.

SMILE!

Puberty can also cause bad breath, which can affect your social life. A healthy smile lasts for life, so it's best to lay the groundwork now with a regular and thorough brushing routine. It can seem boring, but it makes visits to the DENTIST'S CHAIR a lot easier.

MAKE SURE YOU BRUSH YOUR TEETH AT LEAST TWICE A DAY. DON'T FORGET YOUR GUMS AND TONGUE, WHERE BACTERIA CAN BREED.

RINSE

A mouth wash can fight decay and also helps mask any foul smells.

Another helpful hint that battles bad breath is drinking water after eating. It helps wash away bacteria and food and keeps your mouth fresh.

FLOSSING removes the stubborn food pieces.

BAD BREATH WHAT CAUSES IT? IT'S THOSE PESKY BACTERIA AGAIN. THEY BREAK DOWN THE PIECES OF FOOD THAT GET TRAPPED IN YOUR TEETH.

Man TALK

One of the most obvious and embarrassing things about puberty is when your voice breaks. Reading aloud or even talking to friends can be a minefield of high-pitched squeaks—but why?

YOUR VOICE BOX

Your voice comes from a box-shaped hollow in your throat that contains your vocal cords. Air vibrates up through the box to create sounds. During puberty, testosterone makes your voice box grow up to 60% bigger. This changes how you sound.

GULP!

YOUR VOCAL CORDS

Inside the voice box are your vocal cords. These increase in size and thickness and make your voice get deeper. Think of them like the strings on a guitar. When you pluck the thinner string it vibrates at a higher pitch—a little like your childhood vocal cords. The thicker string vibrates at a lower pitch—like your new deeper adult vocal cords.

VOICE BOX

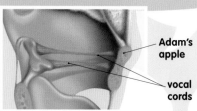

Adam's apple

vocal cords

eek!

EMBARRASSING SQUEAKS

Voice breaking can send out some annoying sound bites. When your vocal cords grow you will struggle to control your voice and it can break out in random high-pitched squeaks. Remember, like playing a new instrument, you're not going to sound perfect right away. And yes, it can be embarrassing, but try to laugh about it, since there's nothing you can do about it. Once your voice box has finished growing you won't squeak anymore.

GROWING APPLES

When your voice box grows, it can stick out from your neck. This bump is known as your Adam's apple. For some boys it is more noticeable than others. Its size depends on how big your voice box grows.

squeak!

GIRL TALK

Girl's voices also change during puberty. It might not sound that way, but they get deeper. Girls can even grow an Adam's apple. However, they have less testosterone, so the change isn't as noticeable.

Growing pains

A group of 13-year-old boys can all look very different. Some are tall, with facial hair and muscles, some are in-between, and some are still boys. Whether you develop early or late, growing up can be a pain.

THE BIG AND SMALL OF IT

The sports field is an arena where differences in size and strength can present particular challenges. During puberty, team sports can pit smaller boys against taller, stronger boys. If you are one of the smaller boys, this can make you stop enjoying sports that you previously loved.

So, what can you do to level the playing field?

GROWING PAINS

You might feel random aches and pains in your limbs. These are known as GROWING PAINS and are common during puberty as you grow quickly. They will fade with time, but if persistent, again, always see your family doctor.

IF YOU ARE SMALLER...

1. Concentrate on **dexterity,** *balance,* and FITNESS—these will be vital as your body becomes stronger.

2. Take up a SENSIBLE training regime to help strengthen and build your muscles.

3. Look beyond the sports field—maybe you have other *talents* like music, writing, or drawing.

Don't worry about size. You will grow and get bigger and better. Be patient

IF YOU ARE BIGGER...

1. You could act as a **LEADER** in your team and encourage the smaller players.

2. If team sports aren't to your taste then try *individual sports* like boxing or track.

3. It might be possible to change your role on the team, while others catch up—this also allows you to learn new skills.

GYNECOMASTIA

Men don't grow breasts like women, but during puberty the surge and imbalance of hormones rushing through your body means you may experience a degree of gynecomastia—growing breast tissue. Don't worry if you do—up to 65% of boys have some degree of it.

What to look for...

The chest area will grow breast tissue—this can be very prominent or hardly noticeable under the nipple. The region can become tender and itchy.

Gynecomastia can be disturbing, but it is only temporary and it will go down in a couple of months to a year. If it persists or becomes uncomfortable, it is always best to see your family doctor.

nd don't give up—you might even hit a growth spurt and tower over everyone.

Keeping FIT

Exercise and sports are great ways to keep fit and healthy. This is important during puberty because your muscles have to deal with your bigger and heavier body. The effort you put in now will keep you strong and healthy as adulthood approaches.

Try a new sport

With boys growing at different rates, sports that you once enjoyed might start to feel physically unfair and less fun. It is always worth persevering, but you could also try something new. How about a martial art, or golf? Or you could try your hand at hockey. There's a sport out there for everyone, whatever shape and size you are.

Hockey

Golf

Karate

Warm up

When you were a child you were naturally stretchy and flexible, unlike your parents. As your body grows during puberty your muscles have more work to do and will tire more quickly. To keep you going on the sports field and reduce injuries you have to warm up and stretch.

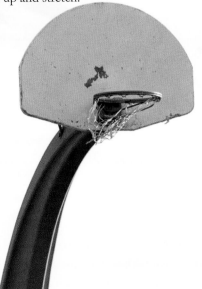

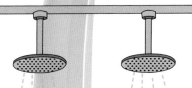

Locker rooms

Changing in front of other boys for gym and sports can be embarrassing. Puberty happens at different times for everyone and inevitably boys will compare each other. If you are worried, you can always change facing the wall. If you are teased and it's distressing, you should tell your teacher.

Stretching

Stretching increases the strength and flexibility of your muscles, making you jump, run, and reach farther. It's important to stretch your back and shoulders, arms and waist, as well as your trunk (torso muscles). And don't forget your legs. Here are four stretches to get you started.

Thigh stretch

Standing on one leg, balance yourself and grab your foot. Gently pull your leg up toward your bottom. Hold for 10 to 20 seconds on each leg.

Hamstring stretch

Keeping your weight on your heels, place one leg in front of the other. Keep your knees relaxed and bend gently. Hold for 10 to 20 seconds on each leg.

Groin stretch

Sit with your heels together. With your elbows on your knees, allow your knees to drop toward the floor slowly. Hold for 10 to 20 seconds.

Calf stretch

Stand with one leg in front of the other. Slowly and gently bend your front knee while keeping your back heel on the ground. Hold for 10 to 20 seconds.

CRUSHES & LOVE

When puberty steps it up a notch, *the way you feel about girls will change*. Your body will start to produce more sex hormones, which trigger new sexual feelings. With all these new feelings, you'll need to know how to handle crushes and deal with rejection.

CRUSHES

A CRUSH IS WHEN YOU HAVE ROMANTIC FEELINGS ABOUT SOMEONE. JUST SEEING THEM CAN MAKE YOUR DAY. SOMETIMES YOU MIGHT DEVELOP A CRUSH ON SOMEONE WHO ISN'T ATTAINABLE, SUCH AS AN OLDER GIRL, YOUR TEACHER, OR EVEN A MOVIE STAR. THESE CAN BE HEALTHY, ALLOWING YOU TO IMAGINE AND PLAY WITH YOUR NEW FEELINGS, BUT WATCH OUT FOR THE DANGER OF CRUSHES.

DANGER of crushes

If you step too far and think it is possible to have a romance with someone who isn't interested or attainable you can set yourself up for being hurt. When you are young and have strong, new feelings it is easy to think they are love. Watch out, crushes can make you obsess about people—you think about them and try to see them all the time. This can be antisocial and isolating. Always try to keep your crush in perspective. When someone doesn't like you back, it is hard to deal with this rejection, even when you are older and more mature.

Sexuality

Most adults are considered to be heterosexual. This is when you prefer to have sexual relationships with someone of the opposite sex. However, this isn't the only path open to you. You might find yourself having strong feelings toward someone of the same sex. This can be a feeling of admiration or romance. Many people have a homosexual experience, feeling, or dream. This is perfectly normal and does not necessarily mean you are homosexual. You are only considered to be homosexual or gay if, as an adult, you prefer sexual relationships with men. You might also hear the term bisexuality. This is when an adult has an equal sexual attraction to both men and women. No matter what you are, it is a healthy, normal part of you, and nothing to be ashamed of.

REJECTION

The people you are attracted to will not always like you back, and vice-versa. This can happen both in friendships and crushes. Rejection is hard to take and it will hurt. The only thing that can help is knowing it happens to everyone and after time it will fade and you will move on.

DOES she like me?

Butterflies in your stomach? Nervous about saying the wrong thing? Liking a girl isn't easy. And feeling like you have to make the first move doesn't make it any easier. But, how can you figure out if someone likes you, too? Here's a quiz to help you read those signs.

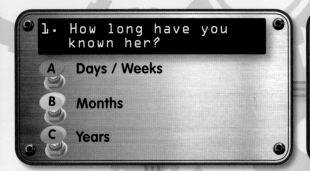

1. How long have you known her?

- **A** Days / Weeks
- **B** Months
- **C** Years

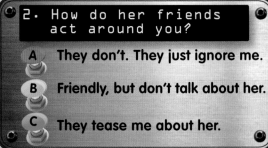

2. How do her friends act around you?

- **A** They don't. They just ignore me.
- **B** Friendly, but don't talk about her.
- **C** They tease me about her.

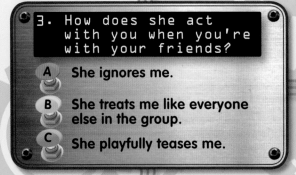

3. How does she act with you when you're with your friends?

- **A** She ignores me.
- **B** She treats me like everyone else in the group.
- **C** She playfully teases me.

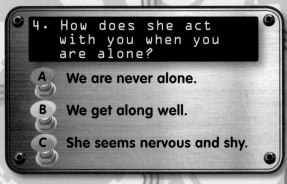

4. How does she act with you when you are alone?

- **A** We are never alone.
- **B** We get along well.
- **C** She seems nervous and shy.

5. When you do talk, what are the conversations like?

- **A** She seems uninterested.
- **B** She only talks about my friend.
- **C** She is interested in what I say.

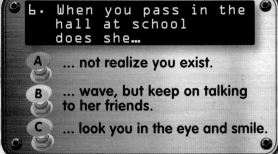

6. When you pass in the hall at school does she...

- **A** ... not realize you exist.
- **B** ... wave, but keep on talking to her friends.
- **C** ... look you in the eye and smile.

FIRST STEPS

It's fine to think that someone likes you, but what's to stop you from being wrong and making a fool of yourself? You have to find out for sure, and to do this you are going to have to talk to her. This might seem daunting, but one way of seeing if a girl likes you is to ask.

You can do this in two ways.

1. Scary as it seems, you could speak to her and find out.
2. A little less daunting is to ask a trustworthy friend to ask her for you, or at least to ask her friends.

RIGHT TIME, RIGHT PLACE

The time and place are also key when finding out, or telling a girl you like her. You don't want to get off on the wrong foot and embarrass her in front of her friends. Try a private place, like at the park or a friend's party.

Just friends
Mostly
Bs
Not interested
Mostly
As
Maybe love
Mostly
Cs

IT'S UP TO YOU

Once you know she likes you too, then what? Well, one thing is for certain, and that's—be yourself. Don't try to change just to gain affection—it won't work out in the long run. Just be friendly and confident and have fun!

AWKWARD SILENCES

Silences can be awkward, but don't panic and try to fill them with the first thing that comes into your head—you might say something you don't mean. Relax and think of something she might want to talk about. Teasing each other is fun, but remember not to take it too far. Laughing together is cool, but laughing *at* someone isn't.

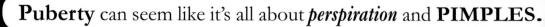

Puberty can seem like it's all about *perspiration* and **PIMPLES.**

"*It's* GROSS!

Mood swings. Your fuse is short and you argue more with your parents and friends.

Voice breaking! Watch out for those high-pitched squeaks.

Zits! Just when you start to hope that girls will find you attractive, these pop up all over your face!

Hairy you. Hairs sprout all over your body and you have to face up to the tricky art of shaving.

Your body is changing and you have no control. You'll need to wash and deodorize every day to stop the stink.

Wet dreams. Embarrassing mornings deciding whether you should own up or hide your sheets.

Spontaneous erections. He pops up when you least want or expect it.

Here are some reasons why it's ***gross***, and some reasons why it's not all *that* BAD.

It's GREAT! "

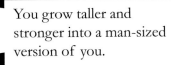

You grow taller and stronger into a man-sized version of you.

Your lower voice is very impressive.

Adulthood—many of life's journeys and adventures begin! One step closer to finishing school! And you get to stay out later.

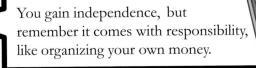

You gain independence, but remember it comes with responsibility, like organizing your own money.

And at the end of it all you can go to college and vote and get your voice heard. Puberty is gradual—it doesn't happen overnight. So, there's plenty of time to get used to it and have fun.

Only a few years until you can learn to drive—no more parent taxis.

✓ TRUE OR

1. Boys may start puberty anytime between the ages of 9 and 14.

2. The male sex organs are hidden inside the body.

3. Boys' voices change easily with total control and no squeaks.

4. Boys can sometimes have erections for no reason whatsoever.

5. Wet dreams are normal and you don't have any control over them.

6. It isn't necessary to wash every day— you won't stink because of puberty.

7. Boys and girls can grow an Adam's apple.

FALSE? ✕

 8 Adults know nothing about puberty and growing up.

 9 Boys all grow at the same time and at the same rate.

 10 Masturbating too much will give you hairy palms and reduce your fertility.

 11 The tip of the penis is the most sensitive part.

 12 Testosterone makes you grow body hair, bigger muscles, and gives you a deeper voice.

 13 …but, testosterone has no affect on your mood.

 GRRRRR

 **14** Boys turn into werewolves overnight.

answers: 1. true 2. false 3. false 4. true 5. true 6. false 7. true 8. false 9. false 10. false 11. true 12. true 13. false 14. false

91

Puberty A-Z

Puberty? What does it all mean? It's hard enough to understand what is happening to your body without all these new, long words. Well, here are a few important words and their meanings.

acne inflammation of the skin in the form of pimples.

anorexia an eating disorder in which people limit their intake of food to an unhealthy degree.

bisexual being attracted to both men and women.

breasts the two milk-producing organs on the front of a woman's chest.

bulimia an eating disorder in which people eat large amounts of food, then make themselves vomit.

carbohydrates starchy foods, such as bread, rice, and potatoes, that provide energy.

cervix the narrow opening of a woman's uterus.

chromosomes microscopic structures that carry genes inside human cells.

circumcision the removal of the penis's foreskin for religious, cultural, or medical reasons.

clitoris the most sensitive part of a woman's sex organs, which registers sexual pleasure.

DNA microscopic threads that carry genes and make up chromosomes.

ejaculation the discharge of semen from the penis during orgasm.

erection the process by which blood flows into the penis, making it firm enough to enter the vagina.

estrogen female sex hormone, made in the ovaries.

fallopian tubes the channels that carry eggs from a woman's ovaries to her uterus.

fertilization the joining of a sperm cell and an egg cell to create new life.

follicle the tiny hole from which a hair grows.

genes chemically coded instructions carried by DNA. Genes are passed from parents to children on chromosomes.

heterosexual being attracted to people of the opposite sex.

homosexual being attracted to people of the same sex as you are.

hormones chemical messengers produced by various glands in the body.

masturbation self stimulation of the genitals.

menstruation monthly discharge of an unfertilized egg and the lining of the uterus. This happens only when there is no baby growing.

obesity excessively overweight.

orgasm the extreme sensation of pleasure that usually results from sexual stimulation. Both men and women have orgasms, but only the male orgasm is necessary for reproduction, since it involves the release of semen.

ovaries the two organs in a woman's abdomen that produce eggs and sex hormones.

peer someone in the same social, educational, and age group as you are.

penis the male sexual organ, used to transfer semen to the female during sexual intercourse (and also to carry urine out of the body).

period menstrual period, see menstruation.

pituitary gland small organ attached to the brain that secretes sex and growth hormones.

progesterone female sex hormone, made in the ovaries.

puberty the time when a child's body turns into an adult's body and can therefore reproduce.

pubic hair coarse, curly hair that grows around the genitals.

sebum oil secreted by the skin.

sexual intercourse the activity during which the male's erect penis is inserted into the female's vagina.

semen the fluid in which sperm are carried.

sperm male sex cells, produced in the testicles.

testes see testicles.

testicles the two male sexual organs, where sperm are produced and stored.

testosterone male sex hormone, produced in the testicles.

uterus the hollow muscled organ in a woman's body that holds and protects a baby before it's born.

urethra the tube that carries urine out of the body in both men and women. Men's urethras also carry sperm.

vagina the passage that leads from a woman's uterus to the outside of her body. A man's sperm enters, and babies are born, through the vagina.

wet dream the act of ejaculating during sleep.

womb see uterus

Index

100% me